INSIDE
TECHNOLOGY

ELECTRIC
CARS

BY CHRISTINA ESCHBACH

CONTENT CONSULTANT
Jeffrey Miller, PhD
University of Southern California

Core Library

An Imprint of Abdo Publishing
abdobooks.com

Cover image: An electric car charges at a
charging station.

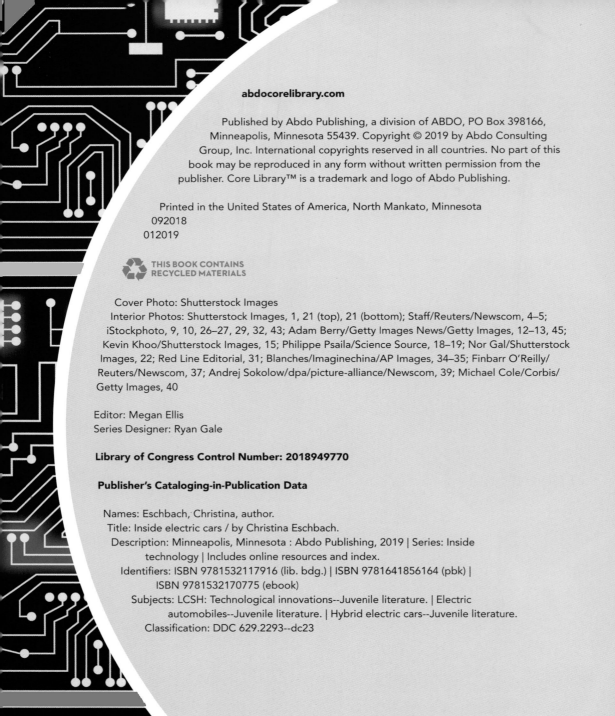

abdocorelibrary.com

Published by Abdo Publishing, a division of ABDO, PO Box 398166, Minneapolis, Minnesota 55439. Copyright © 2019 by Abdo Consulting Group, Inc. International copyrights reserved in all countries. No part of this book may be reproduced in any form without written permission from the publisher. Core Library™ is a trademark and logo of Abdo Publishing.

Printed in the United States of America, North Mankato, Minnesota
092018
012019

THIS BOOK CONTAINS RECYCLED MATERIALS

Cover Photo: Shutterstock Images
Interior Photos: Shutterstock Images, 1, 21 (top), 21 (bottom); Staff/Reuters/Newscom, 4–5; iStockphoto, 9, 10, 26–27, 29, 32, 43; Adam Berry/Getty Images News/Getty Images, 12–13, 45; Kevin Khoo/Shutterstock Images, 15; Philippe Psaila/Science Source, 18–19; Nor Gal/Shutterstock Images, 22; Red Line Editorial, 31; Blanches/Imaginechina/AP Images, 34–35; Finbarr O'Reilly/Reuters/Newscom, 37; Andrej Sokolow/dpa/picture-alliance/Newscom, 39; Michael Cole/Corbis/Getty Images, 40

Editor: Megan Ellis
Series Designer: Ryan Gale

Library of Congress Control Number: 2018949770

Publisher's Cataloging-in-Publication Data

Names: Eschbach, Christina, author.
Title: Inside electric cars / by Christina Eschbach.
Description: Minneapolis, Minnesota : Abdo Publishing, 2019 | Series: Inside technology | Includes online resources and index.
Identifiers: ISBN 9781532117916 (lib. bdg.) | ISBN 9781641856164 (pbk) | ISBN 9781532170775 (ebook)
Subjects: LCSH: Technological innovations--Juvenile literature. | Electric automobiles--Juvenile literature. | Hybrid electric cars--Juvenile literature.
Classification: DDC 629.2293--dc23

CONTENTS

THE FUTURE OF CARS

A crowd of people sat in a large airplane hangar in November 2017. It was dark. Suddenly, a garage door opened. Spotlights appeared in the night sky. Two large silver semitrucks, or semis, drove in. They parked in front of the audience. Elon Musk, the CEO of electric car company Tesla, stepped out from the cab of the truck. He introduced the Tesla Semi. The audience cheered.

The Tesla Semi is the first all-electric semi. Most semis are large and bulky. They run on fossil fuels such as diesel. They pollute the air.

Tesla revealed its semi in November 2017 in Hawthorne, California.

The average semi drives 45,000 miles (72,400 km) in one year. It can get 6.5 miles (10.5 km) per gallon of fuel. That means a truck will use almost 7,000 gallons of fuel in one year! But the Tesla Semi is an electric vehicle. It can go 500 miles (800 km) on a single charge. Electric vehicles use a battery to power an electric motor. They don't run on fossil fuels. They also don't pollute the air.

Musk had another surprise. The semi took a final lap around the airplane hangar.

HISTORY OF TESLA

Tesla was founded in 2003 by five people including Elon Musk. They named the company after the inventor Nikola Tesla. Tesla made important discoveries in the field of electricity in the late 1800s and early 1900s. The founders wanted to create electric vehicles that could match or beat gas-powered cars. Tesla debuted its first car in 2008. The first model could travel 245 miles (394 km) on a single charge. Its top speed was 125 miles per hour (200 km/h). This range and speed were similar to a gas-powered car. Since then, Tesla has created more models of electric vehicles that are similar to gas-powered cars.

Lights turned off. Rock music played. Smoke filled the air. A ramp dropped from the back of the semi. Inside the truck, headlights blinked on. Lights slowly lit up the stage. A sleek red car rolled down the ramp. It drove across the stage. The new Tesla Roadster had arrived.

The Tesla Roadster is a sporty convertible. It has a glass top. It can go from 0 to 60 mph (0 to 96 km/h) in just 1.9 seconds. The Roadster can go over 250 mph (400 km/h). Like the Tesla Semi, it is an electric vehicle.

From semis to sports cars, electric vehicles are becoming more and more popular. But electric vehicles are not a new development. They have been around since the beginning of the automobile age.

THE FIRST ELECTRIC CARS

William Morrison invented the first successful electric car in 1890 in Des Moines, Iowa. Other early cars were powered by gasoline or steam. But electric cars were the most popular. They were quiet and easy to fix.

Then Henry Ford introduced the Model T in 1908. It ran on gasoline. It became popular for many reasons. The Model T was cheaper than an electric car. It was $650. An electric car was $1,750. In 2018, this would be the difference between $17,000 and $45,000. Additionally, gasoline was cheap and available because of oil wells in Texas. Roads began to connect cities. People traveled more. They needed to refuel. Filling stations with gasoline began to spread. But electricity

POPULAR ELECTRIC CARS

There are many types of electric cars available. Three popular types are the Nissan Leaf, the Chevy Bolt, and the Tesla Model S. The Nissan Leaf costs approximately $30,000. But it can only travel approximately 150 miles (240 km) on a single charge. The Chevy Bolt is more expensive. It costs approximately $40,000. It has a range of about 240 miles (380 km). The Tesla Model S is the most expensive electric car. It costs approximately $70,000. However, it also has the longest range. It can go about 335 miles (540 km) on a single charge.

The Model T was produced from 1908 to 1927.

was rare in rural parts of the country. By 1935, electric vehicles had died out.

People became interested in electric cars again in the 1970s. There were gasoline shortages in the United States. A group of countries in the Middle East stopped sending oil to the United States. They did this for political reasons. This made gasoline hard to get. It was also very expensive. People had to use less gasoline. This inspired people to look into electric cars again. As a result, Congress passed the Electric and Hybrid

Emissions leave a gas-powered car from its tailpipe.

Vehicle Research, Development, and Demonstration Act of 1976. This allowed the US Department of Energy to fund research into electric cars. But these electric cars were not good alternatives to gas-powered cars. They were not as fast. They needed to be charged after about 40 miles (64 km). Gas-powered cars remained the most popular.

COMING BACK TO STAY

In the 1990s, people became concerned about emissions from gas-powered cars. These emissions are one cause of climate change. The US Congress passed amendments to the Clean Air Act in 1990. This law aimed to decrease air pollution. Electric cars do not produce emissions. This made them a great alternative to gas-powered cars. Researchers started to develop better electric cars.

However, making batteries for electric cars was tough. Electric cars needed to match the range of gas-powered cars. This would make them more useful. Batteries needed to store a lot of energy. They also needed to be cheap and safe.

FURTHER EVIDENCE

Chapter One talked about the history of electric vehicles, including the Tesla Semi. Identify one of the chapter's main points. What evidence does the author provide to support this point? The website at the link below also discusses this event. Find a quote on this website that supports the main point you identified. Does the quote support an existing piece of evidence in the chapter? Or does it offer a new piece of evidence?

TESLA UNVEILS ITS ELECTRIC "SEMI" TRUCK, AND ADDS A ROADSTER
abdocorelibrary.com/inside-electric-cars

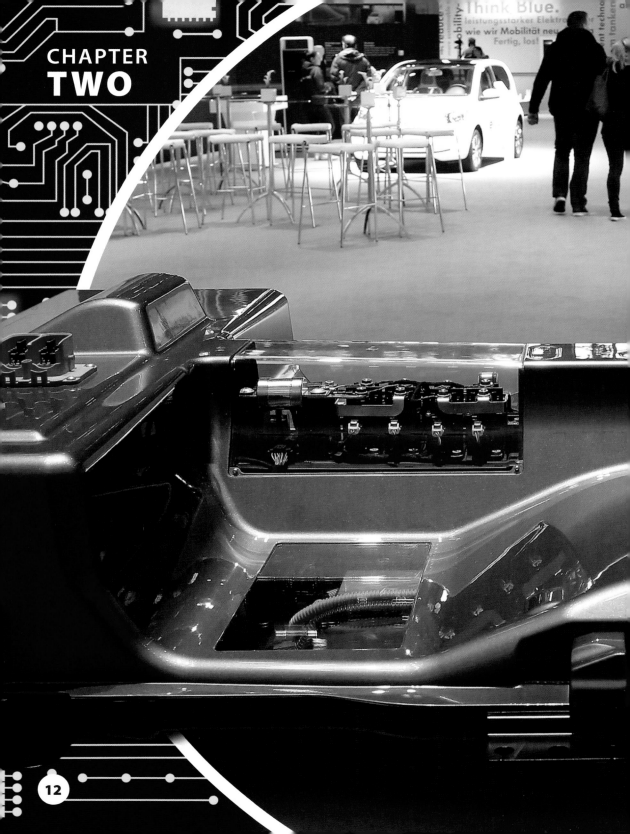

BATTERIES

Electric cars are powered by large batteries. Batteries store energy. There are many types of batteries. But most batteries have a few things in common. Each type uses a set of chemicals and metals to store energy in the form of electricity. Batteries have two parts called electrodes. One has a positive charge. The other has a negative charge. Chemical reactions cause electrons to move between the electrodes. An electron is a negatively charged particle. This movement is called electricity.

Some batteries are used only once. The electrons flow in one direction. The chemical reaction stops when both sides

Volkswagen displayed the battery of its e-Up! electric car at an event in Berlin, Germany, in 2014.

have the same number of electrons. The battery is "dead." But a rechargeable battery can be used many times. The battery is plugged in to a power source. The power source provides energy to reverse the electrons. It returns them to the negative side. Many devices such as cell phones, laptops, and electric cars use rechargeable batteries.

ENVIRONMENTAL IMPACTS

Gas-powered vehicles make emissions known as greenhouse gases. This causes pollution. Electric cars do not produce pollution. However, the process of making and recharging lithium-ion batteries does. Coal is a nonrenewable energy source. It is burned to create electricity. This electricity helps create batteries. It also charges the batteries. This process produces emissions. However, the process of making lithium-ion batteries only produces one half the amount of greenhouse gases as a gas-powered vehicle.

LITHIUM-ION BATTERIES

Lithium-ion batteries are a popular type of battery used today. The positive electrode is made from a dark blue chemical called

Lithium-ion batteries are also used in smartphones.

lithium cobalt oxide. The negative electrode is made from carbon. The electrodes are separated by a very thin piece of plastic. This plastic allows the positive and negative particles to pass through. But it also keeps the two electrodes separated.

There are many benefits to lithium-ion batteries. They are lighter than other batteries of the same size. This is important in electric cars. Heavier cars take more energy to move. Lithium-ion batteries also keep their charge well. They lose 5 percent of their charge per month if they are not used. Other types of batteries can lose 20 percent of their charge per month.

BATTERIES VERSUS GAS TANKS

Gas-powered cars can be refueled in minutes. The average car in the United States gets 25 miles (40 km) per gallon. It can travel approximately 300 miles (480 km) per tank of gas.

A Tesla Model S uses a 90 kilowatt-hour (kWh) battery. It can travel up to 335 miles (540 km) on a charge. But it takes ten hours to fully recharge. There are also fewer charging stations than gas stations. This makes it difficult to travel long distances.

However, there are some disadvantages to lithium-ion batteries. They are sensitive to heat. Heat causes the battery to break down. This can make them dangerous. In very rare cases, lithium-ion batteries have caught on fire.

BATTERIES IN ELECTRIC CARS

Batteries in electric cars are often built into

the floor. They are located below the seats. They are almost as long as the car. They are also very heavy. They can weigh hundreds of pounds.

The battery is made up of several modules. These modules are further divided into cells. Cells are the basic unit of the battery. One type of Tesla battery has 7,104 total cells. But packing all that power into a small place creates safety issues. Tesla takes several safety measures to prevent fires. The battery is placed inside a steel case. Sensors keep track of its temperature. If sensors detect high temperatures, the battery is disconnected.

EXPLORE ONLINE

Chapter Two talks about batteries. The article at the website below goes into more depth on this topic. Does the article answer any of the questions you had about how batteries and electricity work?

SCIENCE OF ELECTRICITY BASICS
abdocorelibrary.com/inside-electric-cars

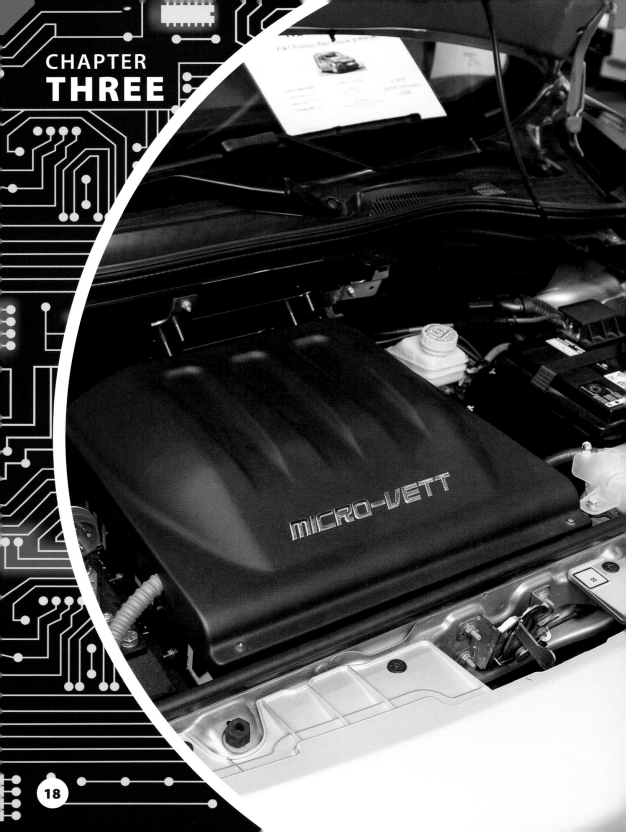

ELECTRIC MOTORS

Motors are very important in electric cars. They help the car run on electricity. Motors come in many shapes and sizes. Some toys use tiny motors. Electric vehicles use large ones. All motors have magnets in them.

FROM THE BATTERY TO THE WHEELS

In a gas-powered car, the battery uses just enough electricity to start the engine. Then the car is powered by the engine. The battery is also used for devices inside the car such as the radio and the lights. But in an electric car, the entire car is powered by the electricity stored

The electric motor in the Fiat Fiorino takes the place of the gas-powered combustion engine.

INTERNAL COMBUSTION ENGINES

Many gas-powered cars use an internal combustion engine. It mixes gasoline with air. A piston compresses the mixture in a cylinder. A spark ignites when the piston returns to the top. This creates a small, powerful explosion. The explosion creates energy for the car. This energy is then transferred to the battery.

However, the force of the explosion also pushes fumes out of the tailpipe into the air outside. These fumes contain pollutants.

in the battery. The battery provides power to the motor.

A device called an inverter sits between the battery and the motor in an electric vehicle. Charging stations charge the battery with one type of electricity. But the electric motor needs a different type of electricity to power the car. The inverter changes the electricity into a type that the electric vehicle can use. The inverter can also change the frequency of the electric power. This controls the motor's speed.

MOTORS AND
ENGINES

Vehicles can use both motors and engines. An engine uses fuel such as gasoline to power the car. A motor uses electricity to do the same thing. In an electric car, electricity stored in the battery provides energy to the motor. The inverter changes the current from DC to AC. In a gas-powered car, fuel from the gas tank powers the internal combustion engine. This provides energy to a battery used to power lights, the radio, and other things. Look at the diagram below. How does it help you understand the difference between electric motors and internal combustion engines?

Electric Vehicle

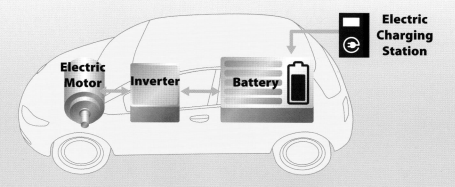

Electric Motor | Inverter | Battery | Electric Charging Station

Gas-powered Vehicle

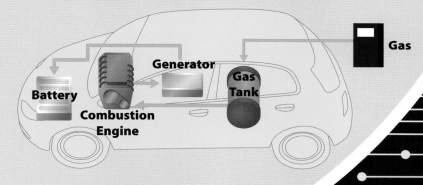

Battery | Combustion Engine | Generator | Gas Tank | Gas

Once the motor is spinning, the motion must be sent to the wheels. A device called a gearbox does this. Gears in the gearbox bring the rotation from the motor to the axle. The axle connects to the wheels. As the axle turns, the wheels turn. This moves the car.

SPECIAL FEATURES

Electric motors have special features that aren't found in gas-powered engines. One of these features is regenerative braking. Gas-powered cars waste energy when they brake. But electric vehicles can use this

HYBRID CARS

Hybrid cars have both an internal combustion engine and an electric motor. This helps save fuel. Hybrid cars can shut off the engine when the car is stopped. They also use the electric motor and batteries at low speeds. Hybrid cars can travel farther than both gas-powered cars and electric cars. For example, the Chevy Volt has a combined range of about 470 miles (760 km) on a full charge and a full tank of gas.

The brake pedal, *left*, is used to slow down the car. In electric cars, this can also help recharge the battery.

energy when the car slows down. The motor runs backward when the brakes are applied. This causes the motor to generate electricity. The energy is stored in the battery for future use.

Electric cars also have instant torque. Torque is a twisting force. It causes rotation. The faster a wheel rotates, the faster the car moves. Gas-powered cars use an internal combustion engine and gasoline to create energy. In a gas-powered car the engine takes time to reach maximum torque. The engine speed has to rise to provide energy. But energy is available immediately in the battery of an electric car. Maximum torque is available right away. This allows a car to accelerate, or speed up, very quickly.

STRAIGHT TO THE
SOURCE

Engineer Larry Nitz is the Executive Director of Vehicle Electrification at General Motors. He helps the company design its electric cars, including the Volt. The Volt is a hybrid vehicle. It uses both gasoline and electricity. In an interview, Nitz described how the company decided which changes to make to a new version of the Volt:

> We learned how far we could push some of these components. There were things that we didn't know when we started off on the first-gen Volt and now we know very well. And there were things that we theorized about in the first-gen Volt that turned out to be true, so we continued them in the second gen. For example, the liquid-cooled battery . . . has been key to the first-gen Volt's battery pack reliability and performance. We're thrilled with that configuration, so we've kept that, optimized it and improved it, but essentially kept that for the second-gen Volt.

Source: Charles Morris. "2016 Chevy Volt." *Charged*. Charged, September 22, 2015. Web. Accessed September 5, 2018.

What's the Big Idea?

Take a close look at this passage. What is the main idea that Nitz is getting across? What does his statement say about how engineering works?

ELECTRIC CAR
CHARGING

Golden Gate National Recreation Area

3 HOUR
EV
CHARGING
8am - 6pm

7CPF001

CHARGING ELECTRIC CARS

There are many challenges to face before electric cars become more popular than gas-powered cars. One large challenge is range anxiety. Range anxiety is the consumers' worry about the limited number of miles that an electric car can go on a single charge. If the battery dies without a charging station nearby, the driver is left stranded. Many people worry about getting stranded. An increase in charging stations could help limit range anxiety. The average US driver only travels 29.2 miles (47 km) a day by car. This is well within an electric car's range.

An electric car charges at a station in San Francisco, California.

RENEWABLE ENERGY

Renewable energy is energy generated by sources like solar and wind. Nonrenewable energy is from resources such as oil, natural gas, and coal. The Earth has a limited supply of these resources. Eventually they will be used up. Solar energy is produced by the sun and collected by solar cells. Some solar cells are made of silicon. When silicon is exposed to sunlight, it creates an electrical charge. Wind energy is harvested by using wind turbines. Wind turbines are giant windmills. When the wind blows, the propellers turn. The turbine is connected to a generator that produces electricity. Using renewable energy to generate electricity for batteries is the best way to eliminate sources of greenhouse emissions.

CHARGING AT HOME

There are different levels of chargers for electric vehicles. The levels let someone know how powerful the charger is. Level 1 chargers use 120-volt outlets. These are standard wall outlets in homes and businesses. People can charge their electric cars at home without buying extra equipment. This is very convenient. People can charge their cars overnight. However, these chargers are

Electric cars connect to a power source through a port. This can be located on the front, sides, or rear of the car.

very slow. In one hour, they only provide enough charge to drive 2 to 5 miles (3 to 8 km).

People who charge electric cars at home may use more electricity. This can cost more money. But some energy companies offer deals for people with electric cars. They make electricity rates cheaper at night. This can help people save money on electricity. Additionally, the price of electricity varies by state. For example, in March 2018, electricity in Hawaii costs 32 cents per kilowatt-hour on average. In Louisiana, it only costs 10 cents per kilowatt-hour on average.

ELECTRICAL GRID

An electrical power grid is a network that delivers electricity to people. Electricity starts at a power plant. Most power plants generate electricity with a spinning electrical generator. Many plants use steam to spin the generator. The steam can be created by burning coal, oil, or natural gas. This creates emissions. Electric power plants are the largest source of emissions in the United States. Even though an electric car doesn't produce its own emissions, it often uses electricity generated from fossil fuels.

CHARGING ON THE ROAD

Level 2 chargers use 240-volt outlets. These chargers are common in public spaces. In one hour, they can provide enough charge to drive 10 to 20 miles (16 to 32 km). Some chargers are free. They can be found at post offices, schools, and

CHARGING STATIONS BY STATE

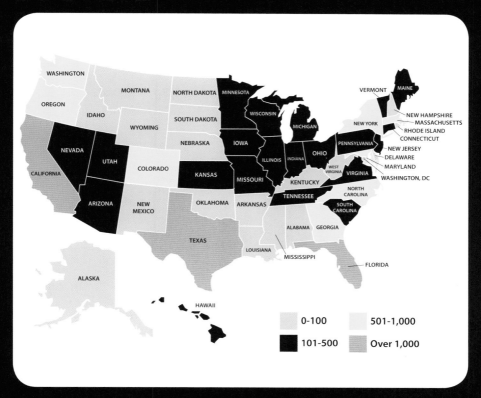

0-100		501-1,000
101-500		Over 1,000

The number of charging stations available is on the rise. But some states have very few charging stations. As of July 5, 2018, California had 4,471 charging stations. Alaska only had 8 charging stations. Look at the map above. Why might some states have more charging stations than others? Do states with fewer charging stations need more?

other public buildings. Other chargers cost money.

They can be found at grocery stores, airports, and

other businesses. Level 2 chargers can also be installed

A Tesla Model S electric car can use a Supercharger station to charge its battery.

in homes. They are expensive. They also need to be installed by an electrician. But they charge faster than Level 1 chargers.

Level 3 chargers are also known as DC Fast Charge chargers. They are in public charging stations. They use

480-volt outlets. In 20 minutes, they can provide enough charge to drive 60 to 80 miles (97 to 129 km).

Level 3 chargers need special equipment in the charging station and in the vehicle. Most hybrid vehicles cannot use fast-charging stations. Additionally, there are over 1,255 Supercharger stations across the United States. They are made by Tesla. They are Level 3 stations. But they can only be used by Tesla vehicles.

As of May 2018, there were approximately 18,000 public and private electric vehicle charging stations in the United States. Charging stations are more widespread than ever before. But there are approximately 150,000 fueling stations in the United States. If a gas-powered car needs fuel, finding more is not a problem. Finding a public charging station is much harder.

THE FUTURE OF ELECTRIC CARS

Electric cars have come a long way since the early 1900s. But researchers want to make the technology even better. In the future, batteries may last longer and charge faster. Electric cars may even drive themselves.

BETTER BATTERIES

Researchers are working on new batteries. These batteries can store more energy. This helps the battery last longer.

Self-driving electric buses called Alphabuses drove through Shenzhen, China, in May 2018. They may be the future of public transport in China.

People also want new batteries to be safer. One recent improvement is a solid-state lithium-ion battery. A regular lithium-ion battery has liquid parts. But solid-state batteries have solid parts. They can store more energy. They also would not catch on fire. These batteries are still in the research and testing stage. They may become available for electric vehicles soon.

Battery company StoreDot has started making a battery that can fully charge in five minutes. StoreDot batteries can power a car for 300 miles (480 km). They use nanomaterials.

THE FUTURE OF VOLVO

Volvo is a car company based in Sweden. In 2017, Volvo announced that all of its cars made after 2019 will use electric motors. Some cars will be electric cars. Others will be hybrid cars. Volvo is the first major car company to move to this type of production. Volvo president Håkan Samuelsson states that this change is the "end of the solely combustion engine-powered car."

In 2014, StoreDot created a smartphone battery that could fully charge a phone in 30 seconds. It plans to use a similar technology in electric car batteries.

Nanomaterials are materials that are the size of atoms. These technologies are also being used in science and health care.

SPECIAL TIRES

Tires on electric cars wear out 30 percent faster than tires on gas-powered cars. Electric cars have nearly instant torque speeds. This causes the tires to be used at higher speeds for longer. The Goodyear company created a tire specifically for electric cars. It has a tighter tread pattern and hard rubber. It is also quieter. Since electric cars are generally heavier than gas-powered cars, the added weight can cause the tire to wear down faster. Goodyear changed the shape of the hollow part of the tire. This change supports the added weight of the car.

SELF-DRIVING ELECTRIC CARS

Electric cars in the future may drive themselves. Self-driving cars use the Global Positioning System (GPS), cameras, sensors, and computers to drive. Cameras and sensors map road lines, other cars, and any objects in the road. The computer uses this data to decide what the car should do next. For example, if a piece of garbage falls in the

The start-up company Drive.ai is testing self-driving cars around Mountain View, California. It hopes to compete with self-driving cars from Google and Uber.

road, the computer can tell the car to drive around it. Several companies such as Tesla, Google, and Uber are testing self-driving cars. But there are many challenges that need to be solved before this technology can be used safely.

Electric vehicles have been around since the late 1800s, but advances in technology are making them

The Robocar, which debuted in July 2018, is the first fully-electric race car. It is also self driving.

more available to the public. With many options for charging stations, cheap electricity, and the potential for self-driving delivery and passenger cars, the vehicles of the past may become the vehicles of the future.

STRAIGHT TO THE
SOURCE

Pat Davis was the Director of Vehicle Technologies Program at the US Department of Energy. He studied the popularity of electric vehicles in the 2010s. In an interview with the Department of Energy, he explained:

> *We think it's a combination of improving technology, new capability to manufacture critical components that we didn't have before, new product offerings, new policy incentives are available that weren't there before, and . . . a heightened sense of our dependency on [fossil fuels]. In the area of improved technology, batteries are two to three times better than what they were just a few years ago, say in the 90's when we had our last run at electric vehicles and the costs for those improved batteries are coming down quick. And in the next five years, we're confident that cost is going to come down even more dramatically.*

Source: Andy Oare. "The Facts on Electric Vehicles: Interview with Pat Davis." *Energy.gov*. Department of Energy, December 22, 2016. Accessed May 10, 2018.

Back It Up

The author of this passage uses evidence to support a point. Write a paragraph describing the point the author is making. Then write down two or three pieces of evidence the author uses to make the point.

FAST FACTS

- The first electric car was invented around 1890. Electric cars were popular until gas-powered vehicles arrived in the early 1900s.

- Electric cars use batteries to store energy.

- Lithium-ion batteries are lightweight compared to other battery types. However, they are also sensitive to heat and can sometimes burst into flames.

- In an electric car, electricity flows from the battery to the inverter. There, it is turned into a form that the motor can use. The electricity then goes to the motor, where it is used to create motion. The gearbox transfers that motion to the wheels.

- Electric cars are usually more expensive than gas-powered cars.

- One barrier to the widespread use of electric cars is the lack of charging stations.

- In 20 minutes, Level 3 chargers can provide enough charge to drive 60 to 80 miles (100 to 130 km).

- Electric cars have instant torque. This lets them accelerate quickly.

- Regenerative braking helps charge the battery when an electric car slows down.

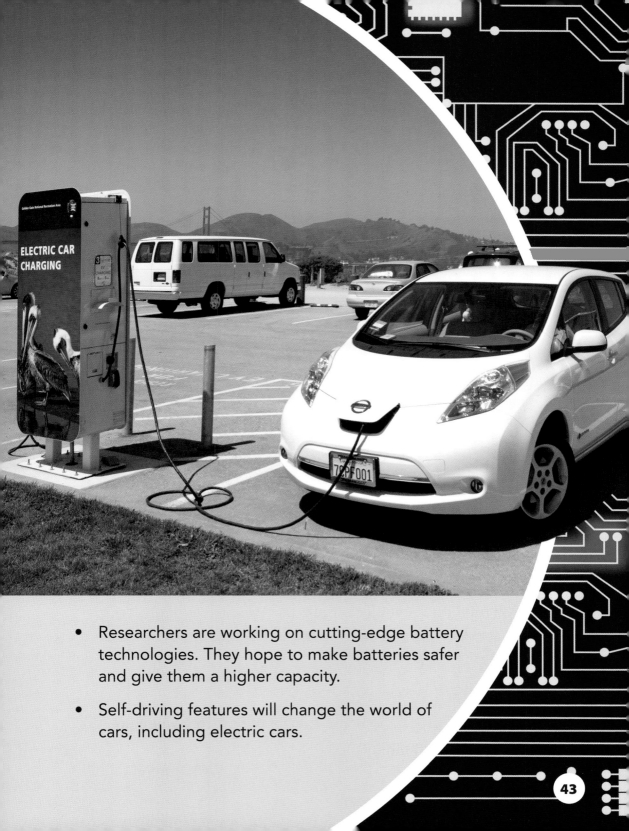

- Researchers are working on cutting-edge battery technologies. They hope to make batteries safer and give them a higher capacity.

- Self-driving features will change the world of cars, including electric cars.

STOP AND
THINK

Say What?

Reading about electric cars can mean learning a lot of new vocabulary. Find five words in this book that you are not familiar with. Use a dictionary to find out what they mean. Then write the meanings in your own words. Use each word in a new sentence.

Why Do I Care?

You are probably not able to drive a car yet. But electric cars could still affect your life in other ways. How would riding in an electric car affect your life? How would more people having electric cars affect your community?

Take a Stand

Some people believe we should continue developing better electric cars. Others believe we should work on more efficient gasoline-powered cars. What is your point of view? Write a paragraph explaining what you think. Be sure to use evidence to back up your ideas.

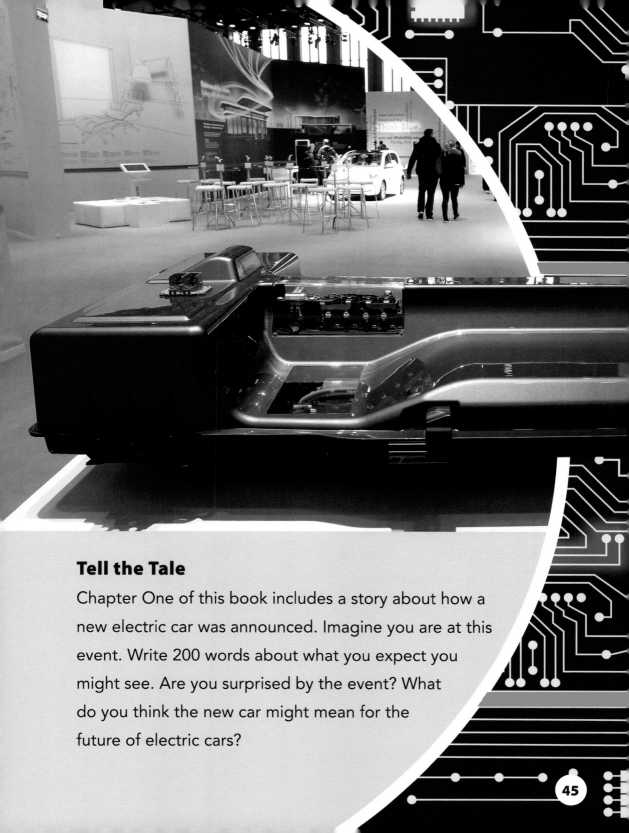

Tell the Tale

Chapter One of this book includes a story about how a new electric car was announced. Imagine you are at this event. Write 200 words about what you expect you might see. Are you surprised by the event? What do you think the new car might mean for the future of electric cars?

GLOSSARY

climate change
a change in Earth's average temperature due to pollutants in the air

electrode
something that controls electrons

emissions
particles put into the air

fossil fuels
limited energy sources made from the remains of plants and animals

generator
a machine that produces electricity

Global Positioning System (GPS)
a navigation system that uses satellites

internal combustion engine
a device that uses fuel such as gasoline to provide power

motor
a device that uses electricity to provide power

rechargeable
able to be charged again

volt
a unit of measurement for electricity

ONLINE RESOURCES

To learn more about electric cars, visit our free resource websites below.

Core Library CONNECTION
FREE! COMMON CORE MULTIMEDIA RESOURCES

Visit **abdocorelibrary.com** for free Common Core resources for teachers and students, including vetted activities, multimedia, and booklinks, for deeper subject comprehension.

Booklinks NONFICTION NETWORK
FREE! ONLINE NONFICTION RESOURCES

Visit **abdobooklinks.com** for free additional online weblinks for further learning. These links are routinely monitored and updated to provide the most current information available.

LEARN MORE

Conley, Kate. *Designing City Transport.* Minneapolis, MN: Abdo, 2018.

Marsico, Katie. *Self-Driving Cars.* New York: Scholastic, 2016.

INDEX

About the Author

Christina Eschbach lives in Minnesota with her cat and husband. She graduated from the University of Minnesota, Twin Cities. She would like to own an electric car someday.